Contents

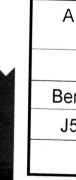
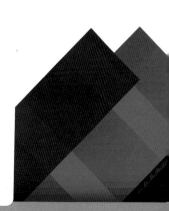

Awesome animals and their jaw-dropping acts

What makes people enjoy amazing animal stunts? Is it because animals seem out of place trying such tricks? Does it astonish people that animals can do some of the same things as humans? Maybe it's that animal stunts seem amusing, unbelievable and bizarre all at the same time. Whatever the reason, we must remember that most animals are capable of more than we imagine. Animal stunts and tricks take time, patience and hard work.

EDGE
BOOKS™

Wild Stunts

AMAZING
ANIMAL
STUNTS

by Lisa M. Bolt Simons

Raintree is an imprint of Capstone Global Library Limited, a company incorporated in England and Wales having its registered office at 7 Pilgrim Street, London, EC4V 6LB – Registered company number: 6695582

www.raintree.co.uk
myorders@raintree.co.uk

Edited by Nate LeBoutillier
Designed by Kyle Grenz
Picture research by Jo Miller
Production by Tori Abraham

ISBN 978 1 4747 0615 5
19 18 17 16 15
10 9 8 7 6 5 4 3 2 1

British Library Cataloguing in Publication Data
A full catalogue record for this book is available from the British Library

Acknowledgements
AP Images: The Bulletin/Lyle Cox, 27, The Repository/Scott Heckel, 17; Gamma-Keystone via Getty Images/Keystone-France, 11; Gentleshaw Wildlife Centre/Katie Smith, 18-19; Landov: Reuters/K9 Storm Inc, 10; Newscom: EPA/Paul Hilton, 6-7, EPA/Rungroj Yongrit, 23, Pacific Photos/Dan Callister, 8, Photoshot, 12, Reuters/Jim Bourg, 24, Reuters/Joshua Lott, 20, Sipa USA/Alex Milan Tracy, cover, 14, 15, Splash News/Solent News, 21, ZUMA Press/Scott Mc Kiernan, 28-29, ZUMA Press/St Petersburg Times, 4-5; Newspix via Getty Images/Tim Marsden, 25; Wikimedia, 16
Design Elements
Shutterstock: antishock, Igorsky, Leigh Prather, Moriz, Radoman Durkovic
Direct Quotations
Page 7: September 14, 2014, e-mail response to author; interview interpreted and transcribed by Yuri Hosono
Page 9: September 15, 2014, e-mail response to author
Page 19: September 15, 2014, phone interview with author
page 26: December 9, 2014, e-mail response to author
page 29: July 20, 2001, The New York Times, "Gunther Gebel-Williams, Circus Animal Trainer, Dies at 66" by Richard Severo, http://www.nytimes.com/2001/07/20/arts/gunther-gebel-williams-circus-animal-trainer-dies-at-66.html

Printed in China.

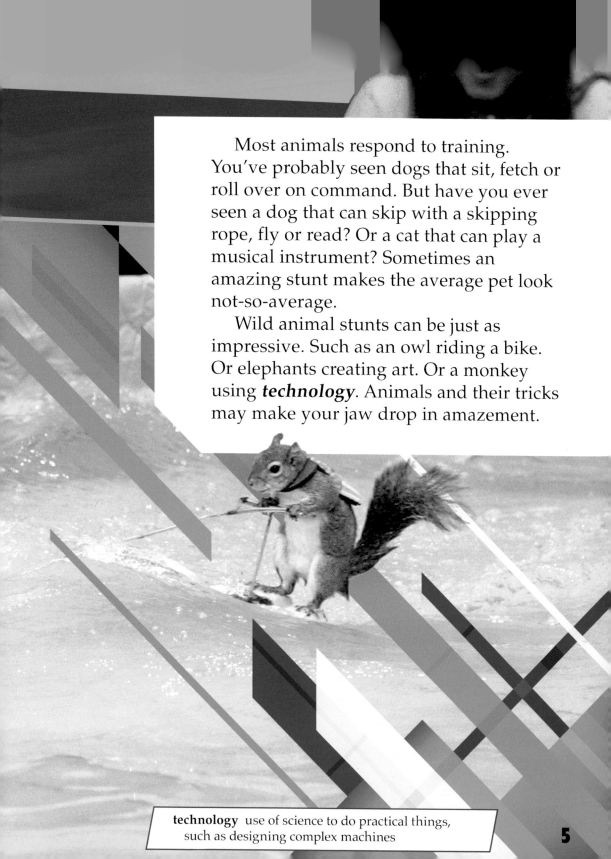

Most animals respond to training. You've probably seen dogs that sit, fetch or roll over on command. But have you ever seen a dog that can skip with a skipping rope, fly or read? Or a cat that can play a musical instrument? Sometimes an amazing stunt makes the average pet look not-so-average.

Wild animal stunts can be just as impressive. Such as an owl riding a bike. Or elephants creating art. Or a monkey using **technology**. Animals and their tricks may make your jaw drop in amazement.

technology use of science to do practical things, such as designing complex machines

Dynamite dogs

Hopping hounds

Meet 13 dogs owned by the Uchida Show Business Company in Fujiyoshida, Japan. They not only skip. They all use a skipping rope at the same time. Yoshihiro Uchida is the second-generation owner of the company. He says that all his employees train the dogs. This way, the dogs learn to trust all the trainers. If one trainer leaves, the dogs still work with people they know. Currently, his company employs five trainers.

CHECK THIS OUT! Uchida's family started a dog circus in the 1950s in order to have work while protecting stray dogs. They've always wanted to help people learn not to abandon dogs.

"Jumping rope is the best way for dogs to enjoy training without using a lot of tools."
Yoshihiro Uchida

After a 30-minute rehearsal, the dogs rest for an hour. This process is repeated a few times a day. Some dogs like treats during training. Other dogs prefer praise. For some dogs, it takes three months to master the skipping rope alone. For other dogs, it can take up to 10 months. Then the dogs need to train for two or three more months to learn to perform together.

CHECK THIS OUT!

Geronimo, a sheep dog mix, can **double dutch**. Owner Samantha Valle trained her for several hours a day for five weeks. One part of the stunt includes Geronimo jumping onto a stick in the middle of the ropes. This is so she'll stay in place. Geronimo's jumping record is 128 times a minute!

double dutch skipping rope game that uses two long skipping ropes swung in opposite directions so that they cross rhythmically

The fabulous willow

A spitz/terrier cross called Willow became better at reading and maths than most toddlers and pre-schoolers. To teach Willow to read, Willow's owner Lyssa Howells chose six words. The words were "wave", "bang", "sit up", "sit", and "Nutrish", a brand of dog food.

Howells started with voice commands. Then Howells used flashcards with her voice. Finally, Howells just used the cards. Willow would do what the card said. The whole training process took just six weeks. Howells used food as a reward.

Lyssa Howells and her reading dog, Willow

"Willow would consistently blow my mind with how quickly she'd pick up new behaviours."
Lyssa Howells

To teach Willow maths, Howells put objects in her hands. When she said either "more" or "less", Willow learned to paw the correct hand, even if there was only one extra. This stunt only took about 15 minutes for Willow to learn.

Willow became famous. She appeared several times on TV and in magazines around the world. Sadly, Willow died in 2013 after surgery to remove a tumour.

CHECK THIS OUT!

Willow lived for 16 years. In dog years, that's about 112 years old.

Mike Forsyth and Cara
in mid-air action

Four-legged flyers

Did you know that dogs can fly? Cara is a
Beauceron search and rescue dog. Cara's owner is
Mike Forsythe, a canine parachute instructor.
Together, Cara and Forsythe completed the highest
canine HALO *parachute* jump to date. HALO
stands for "high altitude, low opening". It is a
term often used in the armed forces. How high
were the pair? About as high as an aeroplane flies:
9,175 metres (30,100 ft)! Both Cara and Forsythe
wore oxygen masks.

parachute large piece of strong, lightweight fabric; parachutes allow
people to jump from high places and float slowly and safely to the
ground

winged suit garment that allows a person to glide through the air
when in free fall, with sections of fabric between the arms and legs
that inflate when the wearer jumps from an aircraft or high place

A dog called Whisper is another high flyer. She rides with owner Dean Potter when he BASE jumps. BASE stands for "building, antenna, space and Earth". Potter wears a **winged suit**, jumps off big mountains, and soars through the air. Whisper rides in a special backpack that has a hole for her head. A parachute helps them to land on the ground safely. Potter first carried Whisper on hikes to get her used to heights. Now Whisper heads for her pack whenever Potter puts on his wing suit.

CHECK THIS OUT!

Dogs have been part of military efforts throughout history. In World War II, the 13th Parachute Battalion of the British Army employed parachuting dogs.

A mutt that marvels

Omar von Muller is a Hollywood trainer who works with talented *canines*. Uggie is a Jack Russell terrier who once had behavioural problems. No one wanted Uggie, and he was on his way to the rescue centre. Von Muller saved Uggie and trained him so well that Uggie appeared in films. In the 2011 film *The Artist,* Uggie won film-goers' hearts by acting out a number of tricks. He played dead, walked on his hind legs and covered his head to appear shy. His lively "expressions" seemed to rival the human actors' best work.

Uggie next to the book he "wrote"

Jumpy, a Border collie mix, is another of von Muller's dogs. Jumpy can wink. He can walk on his two back legs. He can weave around orange cones by walking upside-down while doing a "paw" stand. Jumpy can do high backflips to catch a Frisbee. This amazing dog can also ride behind a boat on a **kneeboard**. He can ride a three-wheel scooter. Jumpy is also an ace skateboarder.

CHECK THIS OUT!

Jumpy holds the record for the fastest 100 metres on a skateboard by a dog: 19.65 seconds. Uggie also rides a skateboard, though he's not quite as fast. He "wrote" a book in 2012 entitled *Uggie: My Story*.

canine of or relating to dogs

kneeboard short board for surfing or water-skiing in a kneeling position

Other four-legged creatures

Phenomenal felines

Cats can't read music, but some can play it. Owner Samantha Martin, a former zookeeper, taught cats to "play" musical instruments. This **feline** band is called The Rock Cats. Though they play off-key, The Rock Cats are believed to be the only cat band in the world. They are part of a circus called The Amazing Acro-Cats. Martin's cats jump through hoops, roll on top of balls, walk across high wires and perform other amazing **feats**.

feline to do with cats

feat achievement that shows great courage, strength or skill

Martin takes in strays and abandoned cats and trains them with a clicker and treats. The cats hear a "click" sound just as they are doing a certain trick or stunt. Then Martin gives them a piece of tuna or chicken at the same time as the sound. In one five-year period, Martin found new homes for 142 of these rescued cats.

One of Martin's cats is called Alley because she was found in an alley in Chicago, USA. Alley holds the current record for the longest jump by a cat: 1.83 metres (6 feet).

CHECK THIS OUT!

The percussionist who plays the cymbal in The Rock Cats is a chicken. His name is Cluck Norris.

Captain Alberto Larraguibel Morales jumping with Huaso

Leaps great and small

In 1933, a Thoroughbred horse originally called Faithful was born in Chile. Faithful was bred to race but was too twitchy and unruly. Faithful was then trained to parade with the army but was injured and nearly died. The army switched Faithful to *show jumping*. It didn't go well until one day, jumping without a rider on his back, Faithful jumped over a wall as tall as a man.

show jumping competition where horses and riders follow a course of hurdles or jumps within an arena or riding ring

Captain Alberto Larraguibel Morales saw Faithful jump. He bought Faithful and renamed him Huaso. In 1949 Morales rode Huaso when he jumped 2.47 metres (more than 8 feet) over a horse jump. Though it took place more than 65 years ago, no horse has jumped as high since.

Feathered and finned friends

Treacle is not a normal tawny owl. Born in captivity, Treacle is now a tame and trained bird. For fun, Treacle rides on the handlebars of Jenny Morgan's bike. Morgan is Treacle's owner and the director of Gentleshaw Wildlife Centre in Staffordshire.

Treacle learned to ride on Morgan's bike when Morgan decided to take more exercise in order to get fit. Morgan liked spending time with Treacle, so one day she put the owl on her bike's handlebars. Treacle stayed put for a 30-minute ride. Sometimes, Morgan takes 16-year-old Treacle to the local woods. For exercise, Treacle flies. Then Morgan gets her exercise by cycling them back to the **sanctuary**.

"If you train a parrot like a dog, then you end up with a dog act."
Clint Carvalho

Clint Carvalho, an exotic bird trainer, rescues abandoned or abused birds. He wanted Kitten, his white cockatoo, to find him from a distance of about 185 metres (600 ft) away. He had no idea if the stunt would work because they hadn't trained for it. One day Carvalho stood on a theatre stage for a filming of the TV show *America's Got Talent*. Kitten sat on a roof 49 metres (160 ft) high across the road from Carvalho. Instead of flying away, Kitten flew straight to her owner! Carvalho considers this the greatest bird stunt he has seen so far.

CHECK THIS OUT! Bird beaks have special adaptations for the food they eat. According to Carvalho, beaks act more like a hand than a weapon.

sanctuary safe place where wildlife is protected

Why fly when you can run?

At the annual Ostrich Festival in Arizona, USA, riders climb on ostriches' backs and hang on. The ostriches race at full speed, up to 43 miles (69 km) per hour.

Animal trainer Steve Boger brings the ostriches to Arizona. He trains the birds for about 30 minutes a day. It takes less than a week to prepare the ostriches for this competition. He doesn't use food or rewards. He just uses "home base", the place where the birds eat and sleep. He also trains the ostriches to pull people in **chariots**.

CHECK THIS OUT!

Tic-tac-toe chickens actually play the game against human opponents. Trained by Steve Boger's brother, Bunky, and his family, the hens rarely lose.

chariot light, two-wheeled carriage pulled by horses

Comet the goldfish shoots for two

Fish with a swish

A goldfish in Pennsylvania, USA, called Comet doesn't perform just one stunt. Not even two stunts. Comet can do many tricks. Comet limbos and fetches a ring. He also plays football, American football and basketball.

His trainer Dean Pomerleau bought a fish instead of a dog. When his children said fish were boring, he decided to train Comet. Pomerleau used a wand with food at the end. For an hour a day, he trained Comet. After two months Comet was a stunt fish!

21

Tame tricks by wild animals

Unbelievable pachyderms

Three-year-old elephants in the Maetaeng Elephant Camp and Clinic in Chiang Mai, Thailand, may learn a special stunt: painting! An elephant called Suda paints a self-portrait. She also paints her name. Other elephants called Bank and Srinon paint trees or birds.

Trainers use food, usually bananas, to reward elephants for doing something right. Sometimes, the **mahout** has to demonstrate the stunt. Then the elephant copies the mahout. Some of these intelligent elephants have learned to paint in just one month.

CHECK THIS OUT! Female Asian elephants stand about 2.6 metres (8.5 ft) tall. Males may weigh up to roughly 5,000 kilograms (11,000 pounds). Even at this great size, elephants can walk quietly.

mahout person who works with, rides and looks after elephants

In the 1950s and 1960s, an Asian elephant called Queenie performed a famous stunt. Queenie water-skied. She performed three or four shows a day.

Born in Thailand, Queenie was brought to the United States as a baby. The Dane family bought her two years later. Marj and Jim Rusing then trained her. Mr Rusing also directed the shows. Teenager Liz Dane always rode next to the elephant to help the playful Queenie pay attention. Queenie died at the age of 59 in 2011.

Suda the elephant paints a picture

Monkey see, monkey do

Dogs are well-known as animals that can be trained. But a company in Massachusetts, USA, trains capuchin monkeys for all kinds of stunts. Monkeys' *opposable thumbs* and motor skills give them a big advantage over other animals. Trainers use a laser pointer and words. They reward the monkeys with praise, treats and *TLC*.

Monkeys are ready for stunts after three to five years of training. They open food containers. They turn pages of a book and open doors. They even know – unlike some humans – how to use technology such as DVD players and computers.

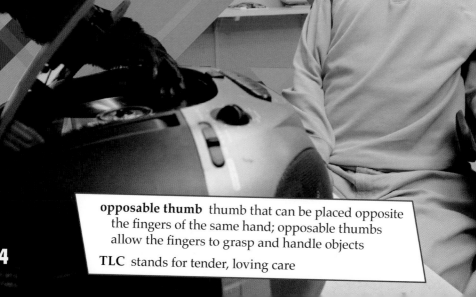

opposable thumb thumb that can be placed opposite the fingers of the same hand; opposable thumbs allow the fingers to grasp and handle objects

TLC stands for tender, loving care

What has four legs, four wheels and squeaks?

Trainer Shane Willmott has trained mice for about 30 years. He started with surfboarding. Now the mice skateboard. Mice are good at both because of their low centres of *gravity*.

Willmott's home-made skate park has ramps and half-pipes. He's even trained his mice to jump through hoops of fire.

gravity force that pulls objects with mass together; gravity pulls objects down towards the centre of Earth

See you at the cinema

Charlie Sammut and his lion, Kaleb, were hired for a part in *George of the Jungle*. Sammut decided to use the "knock-down" training technique for an action scene. The big cat actually knocked down the trainer. The two prepared for several weeks. Kaleb would knock Sammut down. Sammut would stay under Kaleb for as long as possible. When it was time to shoot the scene, Kaleb knocked Sammut down. The director then yelled for Sammut to roll the lion onto his back. Sammut obeyed. All went well, and the scene was used in the film.

Sammut and Kaleb were hired for a different part in *The Postman*. They practised the knock-down technique at home twice a day. One day when Sammut went down, Kaleb growled. He wouldn't let Sammut off the ground. A tractor finally scared off Kaleb. Sammut suffered a fractured rib, cuts and bruising.

When it was time to shoot the scene, Kaleb pounced and growled again. Another trainer scared the lion away. Sammut again suffered broken ribs. He decided that Kaleb's knock-down stunt would have to be retired.

"Many [trainers] choose not to risk doing attack behaviours as it can ruin a cat in the long run, making it aggressive towards all. Instinct can begin to overwhelm training and take over."
Charlie Sammut

Send in the clowns ... and animals

Lions riding on the backs of horses? Leopards jumping through hoops of fire held in tigers' teeth? Elephants strolling through big-city traffic? These stunts and many more were the handiwork of Gunther Gebel-Williams. This famous animal trainer worked for both The Ringling Brothers and Barnum & Bailey circuses from 1968 to 1990. In this time, he performed about 12,000 shows. He didn't miss a single show due to illness or injury.

Kenny was Gebel-Williams' favourite panther. Kenny wrapped his 34-kilogram (75-pound) body around Gebel-Williams' neck. Kenny's legs hung over the trainer's chest. When Kenny died, Gebel-Williams tried the same stunt with Zorro. Zorro was a 68-kilogram (150-pound) panther. Zorro did not like the stunt. He bit Gebel-Williams in the head. Luckily, the trainer was not badly hurt.

Gebel-Williams is credited with changing animal training. He didn't use force or threats. He always used words. By 1990 when he was about to retire, he had worked with 38 horses, 22 tigers, 21 elephants, 4 zebras, 3 camels and 2 llamas.

"Respect is the foundation of my training style."
Gunther Gebel-Williams

Gebel-Williams and his tigers

Glossary

canine of or relating to dogs

chariot light, two-wheeled carriage pulled by horses

double dutch skipping rope game that uses two long skipping ropes swung in opposite directions so that they cross rhythmically

feat achievement that shows great courage, strength or skill

feline to do with cats

gravity force that pulls objects with mass together; gravity pulls objects down towards the centre of Earth

kneeboard short board for surfing or water-skiing in a kneeling position

mahout person who works with, rides and looks after elephants

opposable thumb thumb that can be placed opposite the fingers of the same hand; opposable thumbs allow the fingers to grasp and handle objects

parachute large piece of strong, lightweight fabric; parachutes allow people to jump from high places and float slowly and safely to the ground

sanctuary safe place where wildlife is protected

show jumping competition where horses and riders follow a course of hurdles or jumps within an arena or riding ring

technology use of science to do practical things, such as designing complex machines

TLC stands for tender, loving care

winged suit garment that allows a person to glide through the air when in free fall, with sections of fabric between the arms and legs that inflate when the wearer jumps from an aircraft or high place

Read more

Amazing Animal Communicators (Animal Superpowers), John Townsend (Raintree, 2013)

Animal Heroes (War Stories), Jane Bingham (Raintree, 2012)

Animal Infographics (Infographics), Chris Oxlade (Raintree, 2014)

Could A Walrus Play The Saxophone? (Questions You Never Thought You'd Ask), Paul Mason (Raintree, 2014)

Websites

http://www.owl-help.org.uk/index.html
Learn about the care and rehabilitation of owls who have been injured or bread in captivity, similar to Treacle the tawny owl featured on pages 18-19. Discover what you can do in your local area to protect owls in the wild and how you may be able to encourage them to nest.

http://www.zsl.org/
Explore London and Whipsnade Zoos via the Internet! Meet some remarkable animals, explore different animal habitats, read some hilarious animal jokes, play games and discover how you can help to protect some of the world's most endangered animals.

Index